AMERICAN PROBLEMS

theodore roosevelt

TABLE OF CONTENTS

The Management of Small States Which Are Unable to Manage Themselves

A Remedy for Some Forms of Selfish Legislation

Rural Life

The Progressives, Past and Present

The Pioneer Spirit and American Problems

The Tariff: A Moral Issue

The Management of Small States Which are Unable to Manage Themselves

In the issue of The Outlook for June 18 there was a quotation from a letter of an Anti-Imperialist correspondent, who, in speaking of Egypt and the Philippines, stated that the proper course to pursue was to protect countries of this nature by international agreement, the writer citing in support of his theory the way in which many small powers had their territories guaranteed by international agreement.

The trouble is in the confusion of ideas which results in trying to apply the same principle to two totally different classes of cases. A State like Switzerland or Holland differs only in size from the greatest of civilized nations, and in everything except size stands at least on a level with them. Such a State is absolutely competent to preserve order within its own bounds, to execute substantial justice, and to secure the rights of foreigners. All that is necessary, therefore, is to guarantee it against aggression; and when the great Powers have thus guaranteed it, all covenanting to protect it from the aggression of any one of their own number, their duty is done and the needs of the situation completely met. In such a State the people themselves guarantee stability, order, liberty, and protection for the rights of others. There is not the slightest need of interfering with them, of seeking to develop them, of protecting them from themselves. The needs of civilization and humanity are sufficiently met by protecting them from outside aggression.

There is no analogy at all with what occurs in a community unable to keep elementary order, or to secure elementary justice within its own borders, and unable or unwilling to do justice to foreign nations. The very worst thing from the standpoint of humanity which can happen to such a community may be to guarantee it against outside aggression. The condition of Algeria under French rule is infinitely better than its condition before the French came to Algeria, or than the condition of Morocco at this moment. The condition of Turkestan under Russia has very greatly improved. The condition of the Sudan at present, as compared with the condition of the Sudan under Mahdist rule, is the most striking example of all. In the same way, Panama has benefited immeasurably from every standpoint by the presence of Americans on the Isthmus. Any arrangement which had guaranteed Algeria against the French, or Turkestan against the Russians, or the Sudan against the English, or Panama against the Americans, would have been an arrangement against the interests of humanity and civilization, and against the interests of the natives of the countries themselves.

Moreover, if there must be interference for the sake of the country itself, to promote its growth in order and civilization, actual experience has shown that such interference can only come efficiently by one nation, and not by many. Untried theorists, or even practical men who are influenced by national jealousy and are untaught by the lessons of history, have a curious fondness for trying a system of joint interference or joint control. Americans forget, for instance, that we have actually tried this system and found it completely wanting, in the case of Samoa. We made an arrangement with England and Germany by which there was a joint protectorate over Samoa. The system worked wretchedly. It resulted badly for the natives; it was a fruitful source of bickering among the three Powers. Then we abandoned the system, each Power took its own sphere, and since then we have gotten along admirably; the only trouble in connection with Samoa which arose during my entire administration as President came because we were not able to grant the earnest request of the natives that we should take real and complete possession of our part of the islands and really regulate the government instead of leaving it so much in the hands of the native chiefs.

In the case of the Philippines, there were just two things that we could do which would have been worse than leaving them under Spanish rule. One of these would have been to turn the islands adrift to manage themselves. The second would have been to try to manage them by a joint arrangement of various Powers. Any such arrangement in the case of as rich and valuable islands as the Philippines would very possibly have led to war between the great Powers. It would have certainly led to jealousy, bickering, and intrigue among them, would have held the islands back, would have prevented any development along the lines of progress and civilization, and would have insured an endless succession of devastating little civil wars.

When all that is necessary as regards a small State is to protect it from external aggression, then the great Powers can with advantage join to guarantee its integrity. When anything more is necessary to try to develop the people and civilization, to put down disorder, to stop civil war and secure justice, then a combination of Powers offers the worst possible way of securing the object sought to be achieved. Indeed, under such circumstances it is probably better for the State concerned to be under the control of a single Power, even though this Power has not high ideals, rather than under the control of three or four Powers which may possess high ideals but which are put into such an impossible situation that they are certain to be riven asunder by jealousy, distrust, and intrigue, and to do damage rather than good to the people whom they are supposed to protect.

A Remedy for Some Forms of Selfish Legislation

The August number of the "World's Work" contains an article which is of interest to all who are concerned in the vital subject to which we give the somewhat foggy title of "Political Reform." The article, for obvious reasons anonymous, is written by a member of Congress who, the editors of the "World's Work" say, has served for more than ten years in the House of Representatives, has acted on many important committees, and has been successful in "getting things" for his constituency. The article is described as "showing the reason why the 'pork-barrel,' special tariff favors, and private pension bills become law," the reason being, to quote the words of the author, that "the dictum of the constituency to the Congressmen is, 'Get all you can for US.' There are no restrictions placed upon his method of getting it.... Until the American people themselves become more National and less local, until constituencies cease to regard their Congressmen as solicitors at the National Treasury, Congress will continue to enact iniquitous groups of local favors into National legislation."

This serious charge against the American people—for which there is unquestionably altogether too much justification—the author proceeds to substantiate by relating some of his own experiences with constituents which, however surprising they may seem to the general reader, will seem almost commonplace to all who know how the average American constituency does in actual practice treat its Congressman.

The writer sets forth the fact that, in the first place, ninety per cent of the letters which a Congressman receives are requests for special favors to be obtained in some way or other, directly or indirectly, from the United States Treasury. For instance, while the Payne-Aldrich Tariff Law was under discussion, this particular Congressman received in May, 1909, the following letter from the secretary of a powerful commercial association in his district:

I have been instructed by the board of directors of this association to advise you that at special meeting May 20, a resolution, copy of which is enclosed, was unanimously adopted, urging our Representatives in Congress to use every endeavor to have the present tariff on [mentioning three of the products of the industries referred to] increased one cent per pound and the present tariff on [mentioning the other two products] increased half a cent per pound. I wish to further advise you that we have heard from Senator —— and he informs us that he will take care of this matter in the Senate.

When the bill was finally passed, the Congressman succeeded in adding half a cent a pound to the duty on two of these products and in preventing any reduction on the others. A year later, when the popular clamor against the bill had become acute, the same association that had asked him to vote for increases wrote to the Congressman denouncing the bill as "the most iniquitous measure ever enacted by Congress" and requesting him to explain by letter why he had voted with "the Reactionaries" to pass the bill. When it was pointed out to the association that it had urged the Congressman to obtain an increase of duty on the products in which it was interested, it dropped its demand for an explanation. An influential newspaper published in his district editorially commended him while the bill was under debate for his "intelligent efforts" to increase the duty on manufactured articles in which the district was interested, and a year later the same newspaper in the same editorial column denounced him as one of "the legislative banditti responsible for the Payne-Aldrich measure."

As with the tariff, so with pensions; the Congressman is urged to obtain local favors without regard to National interests. This is illustrated by the following letter, which the author prints, and which was written by the clergyman of a large and wealthy church:

My dear Congressman: I received a call from James H. —— several days ago, and he told me that he had received a very unsatisfactory letter from you regarding his chances for getting a pension. Now, Congressman, while I know he deserted during the second year of the war, yet there must be some way the matter can be covered up and —— be given a pensionable status. He is at present a charge on my congregation. Every one seems to be able to get a pension. Why not he? Do what you can for him, and oblige.

It may be said that this is a unique instance from which it is unfair to draw a general inference. The confessing Congressman answers, No; that he has "hundreds of such letters filed away. So has every other Congressman."

River and harbor legislation is another field in which local selfishness busies itself, to the exclusion of National needs. In this case requests are not made by letter but by delegations which come to Washington besieging their Senators and Representatives. "There is," says the frank writer of this article, "figuratively speaking, between $50,000,000 and $60,000,000 on the table to be divided. The Committee divides it so that every one is satisfied, at least to a reasonable extent." Every one, that is, but the people at large, the people who have no special interest to serve, and who feel keenly indignant that the rivers and harbors of the United States are developed in a fashion so inferior to that of Europe.

Nor are all the requests for legislation merely. One constituent desired to have this particular Congressman put his name on the free mailing list for all public documents. That this would be impossible, because it would mean delivering to the applicant several tons of documents every month, does not in the slightest detract from the interest of the fact elicited by an investigation that the applicant was the manufacturer of an article made from waste paper, and the public documents would afford a useful source of raw material.

Is there a remedy for such a state of things? The answer is, yes; and, moreover, it is a remedy which Congress can itself immediately provide.

There is no complete remedy, of course. No scheme can be devised which can prevent such a request as that of the constituent last named who wished public documents to use in his private paper business. Requests like this merely mean that in every district individuals will always be found who will request improper favors. As regards these people, all that can be done is to create a vigorous public opinion—an opinion which shall not only make it uncomfortable for any man to demand such favors, but which shall cordially support the Congressman in refusing them and hold him accountable for granting them. We must trust to individual integrity to resist such individual and sporadic attempts to corrupt it.

The case is entirely different when we come to the other favors mentioned. These favors are those which the Congressman describes as being improperly, habitually, and insistently demanded by large portions of a given constituency, with at least the acquiescence of the constituency as a whole. It is futile to expect to cure this type of evil merely by solemnly saying that each Congressman ought to be good. It is futile to ask the average Congressman to cut his own throat by disregarding the requests of his own constituents for special and improper favors in the matter of tariff legislation, river and harbor legislation, and pension legislation; even though these same constituents adopt the beautifully illogical position of expressing a great—and, curiously enough, often a sincere—indignation that their Congressman, as the only means of securing for them what they insist he shall secure, joins with other Congressmen in granting for all other constituencies the same improper favors which are eagerly demanded by his own individual constituency. Moreover, under the present system, the small man, when he asks for something in which his own district is keenly interested, is told by the big man who represents the big interest that he can't have his little favor granted unless he agrees to stand by those who wish to grant the big favor—and the small man may be remorselessly "held up" in this fashion, even though the small favor he asks is proper, and the big favor he is required to grant entirely improper. When such is the pressure upon the average Representative, there is certain to be more or less yielding on his part, in the great majority of cases. It is idle to hope that reform will come through mere denunciation of the average Congressman, or by merely beseeching him to reach the height of courage, wisdom, and disinterestedness achieved only by the exceptional man; by the man who is so brave and far-seeing and high-minded that he really will think only of the interests of the country as a whole.

On the other hand, it is just as idle for Congressmen to seek to excuse themselves as a body by uttering jeremiads as to the improper way in which their constituents press them to do things that ought not to be done. The individual Congressman can be excused only by frankly admitting that the fault lies with the Congressmen taken collectively. The remedy is simple and easy of application.

Congress has now, and has long had, the power to rid its members of almost all the improper pressure brought to bear upon the individual by special interests—great and small, local and metropolitan—on such subjects as tariff legislation, river and harbor legislation, and pension legislation. Congress has not exercised this power, chiefly because of what I am bound to regard as a very shortsighted and unwise belief that it is beneath its dignity to delegate any of its functions. By passing a rule which would forbid the reception or passage of any pension bill save the pension legislation recommended by the Commissioner of Pensions (this of course to be rejected or amended as Congress saw fit, but not so amended as to include any special or private legislation), Congress would at once do away with the possibility of its members being subject to local pressure for improper private pension bills, and at the same time guarantee proper treatment for the veteran who really does deserve to have everything done for him that the country can afford. The veteran of this stamp has no stancher friend than the Commissioner of Pensions; whereas he is often the very man passed over when special bills are introduced, because the less deserving men are at least as apt as the others to have political influence.

In the case of the tariff and the river and harbor legislation, what is needed in each case is ample provision for a commission of the highest possible grade, composed of men who thoroughly know the subject, and who possess every attribute required for the performance of the great and difficult task of framing in outline the legislation that the country, as distinguished from special interests, really needs. These men, from the very nature of the case, will be wholly free from the local pressure of special interests so keenly felt by every man who is dependent upon the vote of a particular district every two years for his continuance in public life. Such a river and harbor commission could report, and probably would report, a great and comprehensive National scheme for river and harbor improvements fit to be considered by the people as a whole upon its merits, and not dependent for enactment into law upon a system of log-rolling designed to placate special interests which are powerful in each of many score Congressional districts. Such a tariff commission could get at the facts of labor cost here and abroad by expert inquiry, and not by the acceptance of interested testimony; such a commission could consider dispassionately the probable effect upon the entire social and economic body of all changes in any given branch of the tariff, and its recommendations would represent the exercise of careful judgment from a disinterested standpoint. Such a commission could work in harmony with the Commissioner of Labor, so as to insure that the laborers for whom the tariff is passed get the full benefit of it; for the major part of the benefit of a protective tariff should unquestionably go to the wage-workers.

Even under such conditions of tariff-making errors might be committed, but they would be merely those errors of disinterested judgment incidental to every kind of public or, for the matter of that, private effort, and the work would not be hampered from the beginning by the need of gratifying private selfishness.

It is only in this way that tariff legislation, river and harbor legislation, and pension legislation can be treated from the standpoint of principle and not from the very low standpoint of privilege and preference. The obstacle hitherto to the adoption of such a method of treatment has come from the queer dislike felt by so many Congressional leaders to a course of action which they (quite unjustifiably) feel would in some way be a limitation of their powers. I think this feeling is passing. It is simply another instance of the kind of feeling which makes some executives suspicious about delegating their work to any subordinate, and which makes many voters, who have not pondered the matter deeply, desire to elect great numbers of people on a ticket of such length that it is out of the question for any except professional politicians to know much about them.

As soon as business becomes at all complex—and nothing can be more complex than the business of a Nation of a hundred million people—it can only be performed by delegating to experts the duty of dealing with all that can properly be delegated. It is only by such delegation that it is possible to secure the proper consideration of the exceedingly important business which cannot properly be delegated. The voters, as a whole, for instance, must necessarily declare directly upon all really vital issues, and they should do this when the issue is a man just as much as when the issue is one of legislation. Indeed, in my judgment, there are certain matters, as to which the voters do not at present have the chance of thus acting directly, where it is important that the chance be given them. But they can only exercise such choice with wisdom and benefit where it is vitally necessary to exercise it, on condition of not being confused by the requirement of exercising it in the great multitude of cases where there is no such necessity, and where they can with advantage delegate the duty to the man they deem most fit to do the business.

What is true of the voters is equally true of legislators and administrators the moment that their tasks become sufficiently complex. The village constable in a small community can do all his work directly. But the President of the United States can do his work at all only by delegating the enormous mass of it to his appointees, and by confining his own share of the purely administrative work largely to supervision and direction of these employees. When a President appoints a commission to investigate such a vital matter as, for instance, country life, or the conservation of natural resources, he does not abdicate his own authority; he merely faces the fact that by no possibility can he himself do this important piece of work as well as the experts whom he appoints to devote their whole time to that purpose. Now, Congress can with wisdom act in such matters of prime legislative importance as the tariff and river and harbor improvement, in the same way that the President acts in such matters of prime administrative importance as country life and conservation. It no more represents abdication of power on the part of Congress to appoint a first-class Tariff Commission than it represents abdication of power on the part of the President to appoint a first-class Country Life or Conservation Commission, or than it represents abdication of power on the part of voters to elect as Governor a man to whom they give all possible power to do his work well. In each case the body delegating the authority, so far from abdicating the power, has secured its wise use by intrusting it to a man or men especially equipped thus to use it well, and this man, or these men, can in turn be held to the most rigid accountability if it is not well used, in the exclusive service of the people as a whole.

Rural Life

There are no two public questions of more vital importance to the future of this country than the problem of Conservation and the problem of the betterment of country life. Moreover, these two problems are really interdependent, for neither of them can be successfully solved save on condition that there is at least a measurable success in the effort to solve the other. In any great country the prime physical asset—the physical asset more valuable than any other—is the fertility of the soil. All our industrial and commercial welfare, all our material development of every kind, depends in the last resort upon our preserving and increasing the fertility of the soil. This, of course, means the conservation of the soil as the great natural resource; and equally, of course, it furthermore implies the development of country life, for there cannot be a permanent improvement of the soil if the life of those who live on it, and make their living out of it, is suffered to starve and languish, to become stunted and weakened and inferior to the type of life lived elsewhere. We are now trying to preserve, not for exploitation by individuals, but for the permanent benefit of the whole people, the waters and the forests, and we are doing this primarily as a means of adding to the fertility of the soil; although in each case there is a great secondary use both of the water and of the forests for commercial and industrial purposes. In the same way it is essential for the farmers themselves to try to broaden the life of the man who lives in the open country; to make it more attractive; to give it every adjunct and aid to development which has been given to the life of the man of the cities. Therefore the conservation and rural life policies are really two sides of the same policy; and down at bottom this policy rests upon the fundamental law that neither man nor nation can prosper unless, in dealing with the present, thought is steadily taken for the future.

In one sense this problem with which we have to deal is very, very old. Wherever civilizations have hitherto sprung up they have always tended to go through certain stages and then to fall. No nation can develop a real civilization without cities. Up to a certain point the city movement is thoroughly healthy; yet it is a strange and lamentable fact that always hitherto after this point has been reached the city has tended to develop at the expense of the country by draining the country of what is best in it, and making an insignificant return for this best. In consequence, in the past, every civilization in its later stages has tended really to witness those conditions under which "the cities prosper and the men decay." There are ugly signs that these tendencies are at work in this nation of ours. But very fortunately we see now what never before was seen in any civilization—an aroused and alert public interest in the problem, a recognition of its gravity and a desire to attempt its solution.

The problem does not consist merely in the growth of the city. Such a growth in itself is a good thing and not a bad thing for the country. The problem consists in the growth of the city at the expense of the country; and, even where this is not the case, in so great an equality of growth in power and interest as to make the city more attractive than the country, and therefore apt to drain the country of the people who ought to live therein.

The human side of the rural life problem is to make the career of the farmer and the career of the farm laborer as attractive and as remunerative as corresponding careers in the city. Now, I am well aware that the farmer must himself take the lead in bringing this about. A century and a quarter ago the wise English farmer, Arthur Young, wrote of the efforts to improve French wool: "A cultivator at the head of a sheep farm of 3,000 or 4,000 acres would in a few years do more for their wools than all the academicians and philosophers will effect in ten centuries." It is absurd to think that any man who has studied the subject only theoretically is fit to direct those who practically work at the matter. But I wish to insist to you here—to you practical men, who own and work your farms—that it is an equally pernicious absurdity for the practical man to refuse to benefit by the work of the student. The English farmer I have quoted, Young, was a practical farmer, but he was also a scientific farmer. One reason why the great business men of to-day—the great industrial leaders—have gone ahead, while the farmer has tended to sag behind the others, is that they are far more willing, and indeed eager, to profit by expert and technical knowledge—the knowledge that can come only as a result of the highest education. From railways to factories no great industrial concern can nowadays be carried on save by the aid of a swarm of men who have received a high technical education in chemistry, in engineering, in electricity, in one or more of scores of special subjects. The big business man, the big railway man, does not ask college-trained experts to tell him how to run his business; but he does ask numbers of them each to give him expert advice and aid on some one point indispensable to his business. He finds this man usually in some graduate of a technical school or college in which he has been trained for his life work.

In just the same way the farmers should benefit by the advice of the technical men who have been trained in phases of the very work the farmer does. I am not now speaking of the man who has had an ordinary general training, whether in school or college. While there should undoubtedly be such a training as a foundation (the extent differing according to the kind of work each boy intends to do as a man), it is nevertheless true that our educational system should more and more be turned in the direction of educating men towards, and not away from, the farm and the shop. During the last half-century we have begun to develop a system of agricultural education at once practical and scientific, and we must go on developing it. But, after developing it, it must be used. The rich man who spends a fortune upon a fancy farm, with entire indifference to cost, does not do much good to farming; but, on the other hand, just as little is done by the working farmer who stolidly refuses to profit by the knowledge of the day; who treats any effort at improvement as absurd on its face, refuses to countenance what he regards as new-fangled ideas and contrivances, and jeers at all "book farming." I wish I could take representatives of this type of farmer down to Long Island, where I live, to have them see what has been done, not as philanthropy but as a plain business proposition, by men connected with the Long Island Railroad, who believe it pays to encourage the development of farms along the line of that railway. They have put practical men in charge of experimental farms, cultivating them intensively, and using the best modern methods, not only in raising crops, but in securing the best market for the crops when raised. The growth has been astounding, and land only fifty miles from New York, which during our entire National lifetime has been treated as worthless, has within the last three or four years been proved to possess a really high value.

The farmer, however, must not only make his land pay, but he must make country life interesting for himself and for his wife and his sons and daughters. Our people as a whole should realize the infinite possibilities of life in the country; and every effort should be made to make these possibilities more possible. From the beginning of time it has been the man raised in the country—and usually the man born in the country—who has been most apt to render the services which every nation most needs. Turning to the list of American statesmen, it is extraordinary to see how large a proportion started as farm boys. But it is rather sad to see that in recent years most of these same boys have ended their lives as men living in cities.

It often happens that the good conditions of the past can be regained, not by going back, but by going forward. We cannot re-create what is dead; we cannot stop the march of events; but we can direct this march, and out of the new conditions develop something better than the past knew. Henry Clay was a farmer who lived all his life in the country; Washington was a farmer who lived and died in the country; and we of this Nation ought to make it our business to see that the conditions are made such that farm life in the future shall not only develop men of the stamp of Washington and Henry Clay, but shall be so attractive that these men may continue as farmers; for remember that Washington and Henry Clay were successful farmers. I hope that things will so shape themselves that the farmer can have a great career and yet end his life as a farmer; so that the city man will look forward to living in the country rather than the country man to living in the city.

Farmers should learn how to combine effectively, as has been done in industry. I heartily believe in farmers' organizations; and we should all welcome every step taken towards an increasing co-operation among farmers. The importance of such movements cannot be over-estimated; and through such intelligent joint action it will be possible to improve the market just as much as the farm.

Country life should be as attractive as city life, and the country people should insist upon having their full representation when it comes to dealing with all great public questions. In other words, country folks should demand that they work on equal terms with city folks in all such matters. They should have their share in the memberships of commissions and councils; in short, of all the organized bodies for laying plans for great enterprises affecting all the people. I am glad to see on such bodies the names that represent financial interests, but those interests should not have the right-of-way, and in all enterprises and movements in which the social condition of the country is involved, the agricultural country—the open country—should be as well represented as the city. The man of the open country is apt to have certain qualities which the city man has lost. These qualities offset those which the city man has and he himself has not. The two should be put on equal terms, and the country talent be given the same opportunity as the city talent to express itself and to contribute to the welfare of the world in which we live.

The country church should be made a true social center, alive to every need of the community, standing for a broad individual outlook and development, taking the lead in work and in recreation, caring more for conduct than for dogma, more for ethical, spiritual, practical betterment than for merely formal piety. The country fair offers far greater possibilities for continuous and healthy usefulness than it at present affords. The country school should be made a vital center for economic, social, and educational co-operation; it is naturally fitted to be such a center for those engaged in commercial farming, and still more for those engaged in domestic farming, for those who live on and by the small farms they themselves own. The problem of the farm is really the problem of the family that lives on the farm. On all these questions there is need of intelligent study, such as marks the books of Professor Bailey, of Cornell, and of Sir Horace Plunkett's book on the "Rural Life Problems of the United States."

One feature of the problem should be recognized by the farmer at once, and an effort made to deal with it. It is our duty and our business to consider the farm laborer exactly as we consider the farmer. No country life can be satisfactory when the owners of farms tend, for whatever reason, to go away to live in cities instead of working their farms; and, moreover, it cannot be really satisfactory when the labor system is so managed that there is for part of the year a demand for labor which cannot be met, and during another part of the year no demand for labor at all, so that the farmers tend to rely on migratory laborers who come out to work in the country with no permanent interest in it and with no prospect of steady employment. It is exceedingly difficult to make a good citizen out of a man who cannot count upon some steadiness and continuity in the work which means to him his livelihood. Economic conditions on the farm—in variety and kind of crop-growing, especially as distributed in time, and in housing for the men—must be so shaped as to render it possible for the man who labors for the farmer to be steadily employed under conditions which foster his self-respect and tend for his development.

Above all, the conditions of farm life must always be shaped with a view to the welfare of the farmer's wife and the farm laborer's wife, quite as much as to the welfare of the farmer and the farm laborer. To have the woman a mere drudge is at least as bad as to have the man a mere drudge. It is every whit as important to introduce new machines to economize her labor within the house, as it is to introduce machinery to increase the effectiveness of his labor outside the house. I have not the slightest sympathy with any movement which looks to excusing men and women for the non-performance of duty and fixes attention only on rights and not on duties. The woman who shirks her duty as housewife, as mother, is a contemptible creature; just as the corresponding man is a contemptible creature. But the welfare of the woman is even more important than the welfare of the man; for the mother is the real Atlas, who bears aloft in her strong and tender arms the destiny of the world. She deserves honor and consideration such as no man should receive. She forfeits all claim to this honor and consideration if she shirks her duties. But the average American woman does not shirk them; and it is a matter of the highest obligation for us to see that they are performed under conditions which make for her welfare and happiness and for the welfare and happiness of the children she brings into the world.

The Progressives, Past and Present

There have been two great crises in our country's history: first when it was formed, and then again when it was perpetuated. The formative period included not merely the Revolutionary War, but the creation and adoption of the Constitution and the first dozen years of work under it. Then came sixty years during which we spread across the continent—years of vital growth, but of growth without rather than growth within. Then came the time of stress and strain which culminated in the Civil War, the period of terrible struggle upon the issue of which depended the justification of all that we had done earlier, and which marked the second great period of growth and development within. The name of John Brown will be forever associated with this second period of the Nation's history; and Kansas was the theater upon which the first act of the second of our great National life dramas was played. It was the result of the struggle in Kansas which determined that our country should be in deed as well as in name devoted to both union and freedom, that the great experiment of democratic government on a national scale should succeed and not fail. It was a heroic struggle; and, as is inevitable with all such struggles, it had also a dark and a terrible side. Very much was done of good, and much, also, of evil; and, as was inevitable in such a period of revolution, often the same man did both good and evil. For our great good fortune as a nation, we, the people of the United States as a whole, can now afford to forget the evil, or at least to remember it without bitterness, and to fix our eyes with pride on the good that was accomplished. Even in ordinary times there are very few of us who do not see the problems of life as through a glass, darkly; and when the glass is clouded by the murk of furious popular passion, the vision of the best and the bravest is dimmed. Looking back, we are all of us now able to do justice to the valor and the disinterestedness and the love of the right as to each it was given to see the right, shown both by the men of the North and the men of the South in that contest which was finally decided by the attitude of the West. We can see the Puritan soldier, the man of the Bible and the sword, embodied again in Stonewall Jackson, just as we see that Puritan embodied in the stern soldiers who warred against Jackson. We can admire the heroic valor, the sincerity, the self-devotion shown alike by the men who wore the blue and the men who wore the gray; and our sadness that such men should have had to fight one another is tempered by the glad knowledge that ever hereafter their descendants shall be found fighting side by side, struggling in peace as well as in war for the uplift of their common country, all alike resolute to raise to the highest pitch of honor and usefulness the nation to which they all belong.

I do not speak of this struggle of the past merely from the historic standpoint. Our interest is primarily in the application to-day of the lessons taught by the contest of half a century ago. It is of little use for us to pay lip loyalty to the mighty men of the past unless we sincerely endeavor to apply to the problems of the present precisely the qualities which in other crises enabled the men of that day to meet those crises. It is half melancholy and half amusing to see the way in which well-meaning people gather to do honor to the men who, in company with John Brown, and under the lead of

Abraham Lincoln, faced and solved the great problems of the nineteenth century, while at the same time these same good people nervously shrink from or frantically denounce those who are trying to meet the problems of the twentieth in the spirit which was accountable for the successful solution of the problems of Lincoln's time.

John Brown stands to us now as representing the men and the generation who rendered the greatest service ever rendered this country. He stood for heroic valor, grim energy, fierce fidelity to high ideals. A great debt is owed to John Brown because he is one of the most striking figures in the mighty struggle which was to keep us forever a free and united nation, which was to secure the continuance of the most tremendous democratic experiment ever tried. He did much in his life and more in his death; he embodied the inspiration of the men of his generation; his fate furnished the theme of the song which most stirred the hearts of the soldiers. John Brown's work was brought to completion, was made perfect, by the men who bore aloft the banner of the Union during the four terrible years which intervened between Sumter and Appomattox. To the soldiers who fought through those years—and of course to a very few of their civilian chiefs, like Lincoln—is due the supreme debt of the Nation. They alone, of all our people since we became a nation, rendered to us and to all who come after us a service literally indispensable. They occupy the highest and most honorable position ever occupied by any men of any generation in our country.

Of that generation of men to whom we owe so much, the man to whom we owe most is, of course, Lincoln. Valor, energy, disinterestedness, idealism—all these were his; and his also was that lofty and far-seeing wisdom which alone could make the valor, the disinterestedness, the energy, the idealism, of service to the Republic. Here again, in meeting the problems of to-day, let us profit by, and welcome, and co-operate with the John Browns; but let us also remember that the problems can really be solved only if we approach them in the spirit of Abraham Lincoln.

John Brown prepared the way; but if the friends of freedom and union had surrendered themselves to his leadership, the cause of freedom and union would have been lost. After his death Lincoln spoke of him as follows:

"John Brown's effort was peculiar. It was not a slave insurrection. It was an attempt by white men to get up a revolt among slaves in which the slaves refused to participate. In fact, it was so absurd that the slaves, with all their ignorance, saw plainly enough it could not succeed. That affair, in its philosophy, corresponds with the many attempts related in history at the assassination of kings and emperors. An enthusiast broods over the oppression of a people till he fancies himself commissioned by Heaven to liberate them. He ventures the attempt, which ends in little less than his own execution. Orsini's attempt on Louis Napoleon and John Brown's attempt at Harper's Ferry were, in their philosophy, precisely the same. The eagerness to cast blame on Old England in the one case and on New England in the other does not disprove the sameness of the two things."

In our struggle to-day we can study Lincoln's career purely as an example to emulate; we can study John Brown's career partly as such an example, but partly also as a warning. I think such study is especially necessary for the extremists among the very men with whom my own sympathy is especially keen. I am a progressive; I could not be anything else; indeed, as the years go by I become more, and not less, radically progressive. To my mind the failure resolutely to follow progressive policies is the negation of democracy as well of progress, and spells disaster. But for this very reason I feel concern when progressives act with heedless violence, or go so far and so fast as to invite reaction. The experience of John Brown illustrates the evil of the revolutionary short-cut to ultimate good ends. The liberty of the slave was desirable, but it was not to be brought about by a slave insurrection. The better distribution of property is desirable, but it is not to be brought about by the anarchic form of Socialism which would destroy all private capital and tend to destroy all private wealth. It represents not progress, but retrogression, to propose to destroy capital because the power of unrestrained capital is abused. John Brown rendered a great service to the cause of liberty in the earlier Kansas days; but his notion that the evils of slavery could be cured by a slave insurrection was a delusion analogous to the delusions of those who expect to cure the evils of plutocracy by arousing the baser passions of workingmen against the rich in an endeavor at violent industrial revolution. And, on the other hand, the brutal and short-sighted greed of those who profit by what is wrong in the present system, and the attitude of those who oppose all effort to do away with this wrong, serve in their turn as incitements to such revolution; just as the insolence of the ultra proslavery men finally precipitated the violent destruction of slavery.

In one of Lincoln's addresses immediately after his second election, at a time when any man of less serene magnanimity would have been tempted to advocate extreme measures and to betray personal exultation, or even to show hatred of his opponents, he said:

"Human nature will not change. In any future great national affair, compared with the men of this, we shall have as weak and as strong, as silly and as wise, as bad and as good. Let us therefore study the incidents of this as philosophy to learn wisdom from, and none of them as wrongs to be revenged. May not all having a common interest reunite in a common effort to save our common country? For my own part, I have striven and shall strive to avoid placing any obstacle in the way. So long as I have been here I have not willingly planted a thorn in any man's bosom. May I ask those who have not differed with me to join with me in this same spirit towards those who have?"

Surely such a union of indomitable resolution in the achievement of a given purpose, with patience and moderation in the policy pursued, and with kindly charity and consideration and friendliness to those of opposite belief, marks the very spirit in which we of to-day should approach the pressing problems of the present.

These problems have to do with securing a more just and generally widespread welfare, so that there may be a more substantial measure of equality in moral and physical well-being among the people whom the men of Lincoln's day kept undivided as citizens of a single country, and freed from the curse of negro slavery. They did their part; now let us do ours.

Fundamentally, our chief problem may be summed up as the effort to make men, as nearly as they can be made, both free and equal; the freedom and equality necessarily resting on a basis of justice and brotherhood. It is not possible, with the imperfections of mankind, ever wholly to achieve such an ideal, if only for the reason that the shortcomings of men are such that complete and unrestricted individual liberty would mean the negation of even approximate equality, while a rigid and absolute equality would imply the destruction of every shred of liberty. Our business is to secure a practical working combination between the two. This combination should aim, on the one hand, to secure to each man the largest measure of individual liberty that is compatible with his fellows' getting from life a just share of the good things to which they are legitimately entitled; while, on the other hand, it should aim to bring about among well-behaved, hard-working people a measure of equality which shall be substantial, and which shall yet permit to the individual the personal liberty of achievement and reward without which life would not be worth living, without which all progress would stop, and civilization first stagnate and then go backwards. Such a combination cannot be completely realized. It can be realized at all only by the application of the spirit of fraternity, the spirit of brotherhood. This spirit demands that each man shall learn and apply the principle that his liberty must be used not only for his own benefit but for the interest of the community as a whole, while the community in its turn, acting as a whole, shall understand that while it must insist on its own rights as against the individual, it must also scrupulously safeguard these same rights of the individual.

Lincoln set before us forever our ideal when he stated that this country was dedicated to a government of, by, and for the people. Our whole experiment is meaningless unless we are to make this a democracy in the fullest sense of the word, in the broadest as well as the highest and deepest significance of the word. It must be made a democracy economically as well as politically. This does not mean that there shall not be leadership in the economic as in the political world, or that there shall not be ample reward for high distinction and great service. Quite the contrary. It is our boast that in our political affairs we have combined genuine political equality with high distinction in individual service. During a century and a third we here on this continent—more completely than anywhere else at any other time—have actually realized the democratic principle, the principle of popular government. Yet during this period we have produced, in the persons of Washington and Lincoln, two leaders who on the roll of the world's worthies stand higher than any other two men ever produced by any other country during a similar length of time. We believe that it is entirely possible to combine equality of rights and at least an approximate equality in the opportunity to achieve material well-being, with the opportunity for the highest kind of individual distinction. Hitherto our efforts towards this end have related to purely political matters; we must now strive to achieve the same end in economic matters.

To achieve our purpose we cannot trust merely to haphazard, easy-going methods with complete absence of official Government action and a too exclusively material standard. These did well enough in the pioneer days when problems were comparatively simple, and when the country was still so large that Uncle Sam could give every man a farm, so that, if any man did not succeed where he was, all he had to do was to move somewhere else. We must be true to the spirit of our ancestors, and therefore we must avoid any servility to the letter of what they said and did. There must be equal rights for all, and special privileges for none; but we must remember that to achieve this ideal it is necessary to construe rights and privileges very differently from the way they were necessarily construed, by statesmen and people alike, a century ago. We must strive to achieve our ideal by an exercise of governmental power which the conditions did not render necessary a century ago, and of which our forefathers would have felt suspicious. This is no reflection on the wisdom of our forefathers; it is simply an acknowledgment that conditions have now changed. If our farmers now used the wasteful methods that served for their great-grandfathers, they would not merely fail in the present, but would work a grave wrong to the American citizens of the future. In the same way we must apply new political methods to meet the new political needs, or else we shall suffer, and our children also. In the same way, when we speak of the "square deal," we include two thoughts, each supplementary to the other. The square deal can be secured in part by honest enforcement of existing laws, by honest application of the principles upon which this Government was founded, by the exercise of an aroused and enlightened public opinion. But in order completely to secure it, there must be whatever legislation is necessary to meet the new conditions caused by the extraordinary industrial change and development that have taken place during the last two generations. The greatest evils in our industrial system to-day are those which rise from the abuses of aggregated wealth; and our great problem is to overcome these evils and cut out these abuses. No one man can deal with this matter. It is the affair of the people as a whole. When aggregated wealth demands what is unfair, its immense power can be met only by the still greater power of the people as a whole, exerted in the only way it can be exerted, through the Government; and we must be resolutely prepared to use the power of the Government to any needed extent, even though it be necessary to tread paths which are yet untrod. The complete change in economic conditions means that governmental methods never yet resorted to may have to be employed in order to deal with them. We cannot tolerate anything approaching a monopoly, especially in the necessaries of life, except on terms of such thoroughgoing governmental control as will absolutely safeguard every right of the public. Moreover, one of the most sinister manifestations of great corporate wealth during recent years has been its tendency to interfere and dominate in politics.

It is not merely that we want to see the game played fairly. We also want to see the rules changed, so that there shall be both less opportunity and less temptation to cheat, and less chance for some few people to gain a profit to which either they are not entitled at all, or else which is so enormous as to be greatly in excess of what they deserve, even though their services have been great. We wish to do away with the profit that comes from the illegitimate exercise of cunning and craft. We also wish to secure a measurable equality of opportunity, a measurable equality of reward for services of similar value. To do all this, two mutually supplementary movements are necessary. On the one hand, there must be—I think there now is—a genuine and permanent moral awakening, without which no wisdom of legislation or administration really means anything; and, on the other hand, we must try to secure the social and economic legislation without which any improvement due to purely moral agitation is necessarily evanescent.

We pride ourselves upon being a practical people, and therefore we should not be merely empirical in seeking to bring about results. We must set the end in view as the goal; and then, instead of making a fetish of some particular kind of means, we should adopt whatever honorable means will best accomplish the end. In so far as unrestricted individual liberty brings the best results, we should encourage it. But when a point is reached where this complete lack of restriction on individual liberty fails to achieve the best results, then, on behalf of the whole people, we should exercise the collective power of the people, through the State Legislatures in matters of purely local concern, and through the National Legislature when the purpose is so big that only National action can achieve it. There are good people who, being discontented with present-day conditions, think that these conditions can be cured by a return to what they call the "principles of the fathers." In so far as we have departed from the standards of lofty integrity in public and private life to which the greatest men among the founders of the Republic adhered, why, of course, we should return to these principles. We must always remember that no system of legislation can accomplish anything unless back of it we have the right type of National character; unless we have ideals to which our practice measurably conforms. But to go back to the governmental theories of a hundred years ago would accomplish nothing whatever; for it was under the conditions of unrestricted individualism and freedom from Government interference, countenanced by those theories, that the trusts grew up, and private fortunes, enormous far beyond the deserts of the accumulators, were gathered. The old theories of government worked well in sparsely settled communities, before steam, electricity, and machinery had revolutionized our industrial system; but to return to them now would be as hopeless as for the farmers of the present to return to the agricultural implements which met the needs of their predecessors, the farmers who followed in the footsteps of Daniel Boone to Kentucky and Missouri. It may be that, in the past development of our country, complete freedom from all restrictions, and the consequent unlimited encouragement and reward given to the most successful industrial leaders, played a part in which the benefits outweighed the disadvantages. But nowadays such is not the case.

Lincoln had to meet special and peculiar problems, and therefore there was no need and no opportunity for him to devote attention to those other problems which we face, and which in his day were so much less intense than in ours. Nevertheless, he very clearly put the proper democratic view when he said: "I hold that while man exists it is his duty to improve not only his own condition but to assist in ameliorating mankind." And again: "Labor is prior to, and independent of, capital; capital is only the fruit of labor, and could never have existed but for labor. Labor is the superior of capital, and deserves much the higher consideration. Capital has its rights which are as worthy of protection as any other rights.... Nor should this lead to a war upon the owners of property. Property is the fruit of labor; property is desirable; is a positive good in the world. Let not him who is houseless pull down the house of another, but let him work diligently and build one for himself, thus by example showing that his own shall be safe from violence when built." It seems to me that in these words Lincoln took substantially the attitude that we ought to take; he showed the proper sense of proportion in his relative estimate of capital and labor, of human rights and property rights. Above all, in this speech, as in so many others, he taught a lesson in wise kindliness and charity; an indispensable lesson to us of to-day, for if we approach the work of reform in a spirit of vindictiveness—in a spirit of reckless disregard for the rights of others, or of hatred for men because they are better off than ourselves—we are sure in the end to do not good but damage to all mankind, and especially to those whose especial champions we profess ourselves to be. Violent excess is sure to provoke violent reaction; and the worst possible policy for our country would be one of violent oscillation between reckless upsetting of property rights, and unscrupulous greed manifested under pretense of protecting those rights. The agitator who preaches hatred and practices slander and untruthfulness, and the visionary who promises perfection and accomplishes only destruction, are the worst enemies of reform; and the man of great wealth who accumulates and uses his wealth without regard to ethical standards, who profits by and breeds corruption, and robs and swindles others, is the very worst enemy of property, the very worst enemy of conservatism, the very worst enemy of those "business interests" that only too often regard him with mean admiration and heatedly endeavor to shield him from the consequences of his iniquity.

Now, the object we seek to achieve is twofold. A great democratic commonwealth should seek to produce and reward that individual distinction which results in the efficient performance of needed work, for such performance is of high value to the whole community. But hand in hand with this purpose must go the purpose which Abraham Lincoln designated as the "amelioration of mankind." Only by an intelligent effort to realize this joint process of individual and social betterment can we keep our democracy sound. We all admit this to be true politically; but we have not paid much heed to the question from its economic side. The wage-earner primarily needs what it is pre-eminently to the interest of our democratic commonwealth that he should obtain—that is, a high standard of living, and the opportunity to acquire the means whereby to secure it. Every power of the Nation should be used in helping him to this end; taking care, however, that the help shall be given in such fashion as to represent real help, and not harm; for the worst injury that could be done him or any other man would be to teach him to rely primarily on "the State" instead of on himself. The collective power of the State can help; but it is the individual's own power of self-help which is most important.

Now, I am well aware that demagogues and doctrinaire reformers of a certain type may try to turn such use of the powers of the State into an abuse. We should set our faces like flint against any such abuse. We should make it fully understood by the workingmen—by the men of small means—that we will do everything in our power for them except what is wrong; but that we will do wrong for no man—neither for them nor for any one else. Nevertheless, the fact that there are dangers in following a given course merely means that we should follow it with a cautious realization of these dangers, and not that we should abandon it, if on the whole it is the right course.

It is just so with personal liberty. The unlimited freedom which the individual property-owner has enjoyed has been of use to this country in many ways, and we can continue our prosperous economic career only by retaining an economic organization which will offer to the men of the stamp of the great captains of industry the opportunity and inducement to earn distinction. Nevertheless, we as Americans must now face the fact that this great freedom which the individual property-owner has enjoyed in the past has produced evils which were inevitable from its unrestrained exercise. It is this very freedom—this absence of State and National restraint—that has tended to create a small class of enormously wealthy and economically powerful men whose chief object is to hold and increase their power. Any feeling of special hatred toward these men is as absurd as any feeling of special regard. Some of them have gained their power by cheating and swindling, just as some very small business men cheat and swindle; but, as a whole, big men are no better and no worse than their small competitors, from a moral standpoint. Where they do wrong it is even more important to punish them than to punish a small man who does wrong, because their position makes it especially wicked for them to yield to temptation; but the prime need is to change the conditions which enable them to accumulate a power which it is not for the general welfare that they should hold or exercise, and to make this change not only without vindictiveness, without doing injustice to individuals, but also in a cautious and temperate spirit, testing our theories by actual practice, so that our legislation may represent the minimum of restrictions upon the individual initiative of the exceptional man which is compatible with obtaining the maximum of welfare for the average man. We grudge no man a fortune which represents merely his own power and sagacity exercised with entire regard to the welfare of his fellows. But the fortune must not only be honorably obtained and well used; it is also essential that it should not represent a necessary incident of widespread, even though partial, economic privation. It is not even enough that the fortune should have been gained without doing damage to the community. We should only permit it to be gained and kept so long as the gaining and the keeping represent benefit to the community. This I know implies a policy of a far more active governmental interference with social and economic conditions than we have hitherto seen in this country; but I think we have to face the fact that such increase in governmental activity is now necessary. We should work cautiously and patiently and with complete absence of animosity, except toward the individuals whom we are certain have been guilty of flagrant evil; but we should also work firmly to realize the democratic purpose, economically and socially as well as politically. We must make popular government responsible for the betterment both of the individual and of society at large.

Let me repeat once more that, while such responsible governmental action is an absolutely necessary thing to achieve our purpose, yet it will be worse than useless if it is not accompanied by a serious effort on the part of the individuals composing the community thus to achieve each for himself a higher standard of individual betterment, not merely material but spiritual and intellectual. In other words, our democracy depends on individual improvement just as much as upon collective effort to achieve our common social improvement. The most serious troubles of the present day are unquestionably due in large part to lack of efficient governmental action, and cannot be remedied without such action; but neither can any remedy permanently avail unless back of it stands a high general character of individual citizenship.

This governmental improvement can be accomplished partly by the States, in so far as any given evil affects only one State, or one or two States; in so far as a merely local remedy is needed for a merely local disease. But the betterment must be accomplished partly, and I believe mainly, through the National Government. I do not ask for over-centralization; but I do ask that we work in a spirit of broad and far-reaching nationalism when we deal with what concerns our people as a whole. I no more make a fetish of centralization than of decentralization. Any given case must be treated on its special merits. Each community should be required to deal with all that is of merely local interest; and nothing should be undertaken by the Government of the whole country which can thus wisely be left to local management. But those functions of government which no wisdom on the part of the States will enable them satisfactorily to perform must be performed by the National Government. We are all Americans; our common interests are as broad as the continent; the most vital problems are those that affect us all alike. The regulation of big business, and therefore the control of big property in the public interest, are pre-eminently instances of such functions which can only be performed efficiently and wisely by the Nation; and, moreover, so far as labor is employed in connection with inter-State business, it should also be treated as a matter for the National Government. The National power over inter-State commerce warrants our dealing with such questions as employers' liability in inter-State business, and the protection and compensation for injuries of railway employees. The National Government of right has, and must exercise, its power for the protection of labor which is connected with the instrumentalities of inter-State commerce.

The National Government belongs to the whole American people; and where the whole American people are interested that interest can be effectively guarded only by the National Government. We ought to use the National Government as an agency, a tool, wherever it is necessary, in order that we may organize our entire political, economical, and social life in accordance with a far-reaching democratic purpose. We should make the National governmental machinery an adequate and constructive instrument for constructive work in the realization of a National democratic ideal. I lay emphasis upon the word constructive. Too often the Federal Government, and above all the Federal judiciary, has permitted itself to be employed for purely negative purposes—that is, to thwart the action of the States while not permitting efficient National action in its place. From the National standpoint nothing can be worse—nothing can be full of graver menace—for the National life than to have the Federal courts active in nullifying State action to remedy the evils arising from the abuse of great wealth, unless the Federal authorities, executive, legislative, and judicial alike, do their full duty in effectually meeting the need of a thoroughgoing and radical supervision and control of big inter-State business in all its forms. Many great financiers, and many of the great corporation lawyers who advise them, still oppose any effective regulation of big business by the National Government, because, for the time being, it serves their interest to trust to the chaos which is caused on the one hand by inefficient laws and conflicting and often unwise efforts at regulation by State governments, and, on the other hand, by the efficient protection against such regulation afforded by the Federal courts. In the end this condition will prove intolerable, and will hurt most of all the very class which it at present benefits. The continuation of such conditions would mean that the corporations would find that they had purchased immunity from the efficient exercise of Federal regulative power at the cost of being submitted to a violent and radical local supervision, inflamed to fury by having repeatedly been thwarted, and not chastened by exercised responsibility. To refuse to take, or to permit others to take, wise and practical action for the remedying of abuses is to invite unwise action under the lead of violent extremists.

I do not wish to see the Nation forced into ownership of the railways if it can possibly be avoided; and the only alternative is thoroughgoing and effective regulation, which shall be based on full knowledge of all the facts, including a physical valuation of the property, the details of its capitalization, and the like. We should immediately set about securing this physical valuation. The Government should oversee the issuance of all stocks and bonds, and should have complete power over rates and traffic agreements. The railways are really highways, and it is the fundamental right of the people as a whole to see that they are open to use on just and reasonable terms, equal to all persons. The Hepburn Bill marked a great step in advance; the law of last session, in its final shape and as actually passed, marks, on the whole, another decided step in advance.

Corporate regulation is merely one phase of a vast problem. The true friend of property, the true conservative, is he who insists that property shall be the servant and not the master of the commonwealth; who insists that the creature of man's making shall be the servant and not the master of the man who made it. The citizens of the United States must effectively control the mighty commercial forces which they have themselves called into being.

Corporations are necessary to the effective use of the forces of production and commerce under modern conditions. We cannot effectively prohibit all combinations without doing far-reaching economic harm; and it is mere folly to do as we have done in the past—to try to combine incompatible systems—that is, to try both to prohibit and regulate combinations. Combinations in industry are the result of an imperative economic law which cannot be repealed by political legislation. The effort at prohibiting all combination has substantially failed. The only course left is active corporate regulation—that is, the control of corporations for the common good—the suppression of the evils that they work, and the retention, as far as may be, of that business efficiency in their use which has placed us in the forefront of industrial peoples. I need waste no words upon our right so to control them. The corporation is the creature of government, and the people have the right to handle it as they desire; all they need pay attention to is the expediency of realizing this right in some way that shall be productive of good and not harm. The corporate manager who achieves success by honest efficiency in giving the best service to the public should be favored because we all benefit by his efficiency. He realizes Abraham Lincoln's definition which I have quoted above, because he works for his own material betterment and at the same time for the "amelioration of mankind," and he should be helped by the Government because his success is good for the National welfare. But a man who grasps and holds business power by breaking the industrial efficiency of others, who wins success by methods which are against the public interest and degrading to the public morals, should not be permitted to exercise such power. Instead of punishing him by a long and doubtful process of the law after the wrong has been committed, there should be such effective Government regulation as to check the evil tendencies at the moment that they start to develop. Overcapitalization in all its shapes is one of the prime evils; for it is one of the most fruitful methods by which unscrupulous men get improper profits, and when the holdings come into innocent hands we are forced into the uncomfortable position of being obliged to reduce the dividends of innocent investors, or of permitting the public and the wage-workers, either or both, to suffer. Such really effective control over great inter-State business can come only from the National Government. The American people demands the new Nationalism needful to deal with the new problems; it puts the National need above sectional or personal advantage; it is impatient of the utter confusion which results from local legislatures attempting to treat National issues as local issues; it is still more impatient of the National impotence which springs from the over-division of governmental powers; the impotence which makes it possible for local selfishness, or for the vulpine legal cunning which is hired by wealthy special interests, to bring National activities to a deadlock.

The control must be exercised in several different ways. It may be that National incorporation is not at the moment possible; but there must be some affirmative National control, on terms which will secure publicity in the affairs of and complete supervision and control over the big, Nation-wide business corporations; a control that will prevent and not legalize abuses. Such control should imply the issuance of securities by corporations only under thoroughgoing Governmental supervision, and after compliance with Governmental requirements which shall effectually prevent overcapitalization. Such control should protect and favor the corporation which acts honestly, exactly as it should check and punish, when it cannot prevent, every species of dishonesty.

In the Inter-State Commerce Commission and in the Federal Bureau of Corporations we have bodies which, if their powers are sufficiently enlarged after the right fashion, can render great and substantial service. The average American citizen should have presented to him in a simple and easily comprehended form the truth about the business affairs that affect his daily life as consumer, employee, employer, as investor, as voter. The issue of securities should be subject to rigorous Government supervision. There are concrete instances of unfair competition that can be reached under the Federal criminal legislation, and they should be attacked and destroyed in the courts. But the laws should be such that normally, and save in extraordinary circumstances, there should be no need of recourse to the courts. What is needed is administrative supervision and control. This should be so exercised that the highways of commerce and opportunity should be open to all; and not nominally open, but really open, a consistent effort being made to deprive every man of any advantage that is not due to his own superiority and efficiency, controlled by moral purpose. The National Bureau of Corporations has not been given the powers or the funds to develop its full usefulness, and yet it offers one of the prime means at the disposal of the people of keeping them fully acquainted with all the facts about corporation control. We have a right to expect from this Bureau and from the Inter-State Commerce Commission a very high grade of public service. We should be as sure of the proper conduct of inter-State railways and the proper management of inter-State business as we are now sure of the conduct and management of the National banks, and we should have as effective supervision in one case as in the other.

Not only as a matter of justice and honesty, but as a matter of prime popular interest, we should see that this control is so exercised as to favor a proper return to the upright business manager and honest investor. In the matter of railway rates, for instance, it is just as much our duty to see that they are not too low as that they are not too high. We must preserve the right of the railway employee to proper wages and the right of the investor to proper interest as scrupulously as we preserve the right of the shipper and the producer and the consumer. We cannot afford to do injustice, or suffer it to be done, to any of these. But in order to do justice we must have full knowledge. We must have the right to find out every fact connected with the business of the railway, so as to base our judgment, not on any one fact, but on all taken together. Inasmuch as it is so often impossible to punish wrongs done in the past, and to prevent the consequences of the wrongs thus committed being felt by one innocent class, without shifting the burden to the shoulders of another innocent class, we ought to provide that hereafter business shall be carried on from its inception in such a way as to prevent swindling. Incidentally, this will also tend to prevent that excessive profit by one man, which may not be swindling, under existing laws, but which nevertheless is against the interest of the commonwealth; To know all the facts is of as much interest to the investor and the wageworker as to the shipper, the producer, the consumer. Full knowledge of the past helps us in dealing with the future. If we find that high rates are due to overcapitalization in the past, or to any kind of sharp practice in the past, then, whether or not it is possible to take action which will partly remedy the wrong, we are certainly in a better position to prevent a repetition of the wrong.

Let me, in closing, put my position in a nutshell. When I say that I am for the square deal, I mean not merely that I stand for fair play under the present rules of the game, but that I stand for having these rules changed so as to work for a more substantial equality of opportunity and of reward for equally good service. So far as possible, the reward should be based upon service; and this necessarily implies that where a man renders us service in return for the fortune he receives, he has the right to receive it only on terms just to the whole people. For this reason there should be a heavily progressive National inheritance tax on big fortunes. The really big fortune, by the mere fact of its size, acquires qualities which differentiate it in kind as well as in degree from what is possessed by men of relatively small means. A heavily progressive inheritance tax on all such fortunes (heaviest on absentees) has the good qualities of an income tax, without its drawbacks; it is far more beneficial to the community at large, and far less burdensome to private individuals, as well as far more easily collected. A moderate, but progressive, income tax, carefully devised to fall genuinely on those who ought to pay, would, I believe, be a good thing; but a heavy and heavily progressive inheritance tax on great fortunes would be a far better thing.

I have tried to set before you my creed. I believe in property rights, but I believe in them as adjuncts to, and not as substitutes for, human rights. I believe that normally the rights of property coincide with the rights of man; but where they do not, then the rights of man must be put above the rights of property. I believe in shaping the ends of government to protect property; but wherever the alternative must be faced, I am for man and not for property. I am far from underestimating the importance of dividends, but I rank dividends below human character. I know well that if there is not sufficient prosperity the people will in the end rebel against any system, no matter how exalted morally; and reformers must not bring upon the people permanent economic ruin, or the reforms themselves will go down in the ruin. But we must be ready to face any temporary disaster—whether or not brought on by those who will war against us to the knife—if only through such disaster can we attain our goal. And those who oppose all reform will do well to remember that ruin in its worst form is inevitable if our National life brings us nothing whatever but a swollen and badly distributed material prosperity. In other words, I feel that material interests are chiefly good, not in themselves, but as an indispensable foundation upon which we should build a higher superstructure, a superstructure without which the foundation becomes worthless. Therefore I believe that the destinies of this country should be shaped primarily by moral forces, and by material forces only as they are subordinated to these moral forces. I believe that material wealth is an exceedingly valuable servant, and a particularly abhorrent master, in our National life. I think one end of government should be to achieve prosperity; but it should follow this end chiefly to serve an even higher and more important end—that of promoting the character and welfare of the average man. In the long run, and inevitably, the actual control of the government will be determined by the chief end which the government subserves. If the end and aim of government action is merely to accumulate general material prosperity, treating such prosperity as an end in itself and not as a means, then it is inevitable that material wealth and the masters of that wealth will dominate and control the course of national action. If, on the other hand, the achievement of material wealth is treated, not as an end of government, but as a thing of great value, it is true—so valuable as to be indispensable—but of value only in connection with the achievement of other ends, then we are free to seek through our government, and through the supervision of our individual activities, the realization of a true democracy. Then we are free to seek not only the heaping up of material wealth, but a wise and generous distribution of such wealth so as to diminish grinding poverty, and, so far as may be, to equalize social and economic no less than political opportunity.

The people as a whole can be benefited morally and materially by a system which shall permit of ample reward for exceptional efficiency, but which shall nevertheless secure to the average man who does his work faithfully and well, the reward to which he is entitled. Remember that I speak only of the man who does his work faithfully and well. The man who shirks his work, who is lazy or vicious, or even merely incompetent, deserves scant consideration; we may be sorry for his family, but it is folly to waste sympathy on the man himself; and it is also folly for sentimentalists to try to shift the burden of blame from such a man himself to "society;" and it is an outrage to give him the reward given to his hard-working, upright, and efficient brother. Still less should we waste sympathy on the criminal; there are altogether too many honest men who need it; and one chief point in dealing with the criminal should be to make him understand that he will be in personal peril if he becomes a lawbreaker. I realize entirely that in the last analysis, with the nation as with the individual, it is private character that counts for most. It is because of this realization that I gladly lay myself open to the charge that I preach too much, and dwell too much upon moral commonplaces; for though I believe with all my heart in the nationalization of this Nation—in the collective use on behalf of the American people of the governmental powers which can be derived only from the American people as a whole—yet I believe even more in the practical application by the individual of those great fundamental moralities.

A certain type of rather thinly intellectual man sneers at these moralities as "commonplaces;" and base and evil men, selfish and short-sighted men, are immensely pleased to see them denounced and derided. Yet surely it is the duty of every public man to try to make all of us keep in mind, and practice, the moralities essential to the welfare of the American people. It is of vital concern to the American people that the men and women of this great Nation should be good husbands and wives, fathers and mothers, sons and daughters; that we should be good neighbors, one to another, in business and in social life; that we should each do his or her primary duty in the home without neglecting the duty to the State; that we should dwell even more on our duties than on our rights; that we should work hard and faithfully; that we should prize intelligence, but prize courage and honesty and cleanliness even more. Inefficiency is a curse; and no good intention atones for weakness of will and flabbiness of moral, mental, and physical fiber; yet it is also true that no intellectual cleverness, no ability to achieve material prosperity, can atone for the lack of the great moral qualities which are the surest foundation of national might. In this great free democracy it behooves all the people so to bear themselves that, not with their lips only but in their lives, they shall show their fealty to the great truth pronounced of old—the truth that Righteousness exalteth a nation.

The Pioneer Spirit and American Problems

For a number of years I have believed and urged the principles I set forth in the following article. Their presentation here is in substance what I said in three recent speeches at Cheyenne, Denver, and Omaha.

The men who have made this great republic what it is, and especially the men who have turned it into a continental commonwealth, have possessed in the highest degree the great virile virtues of strength, courage, energy, and undaunted and unwavering resolution. Their typical leaders—of whom Abraham Lincoln, though the most exceptional, was the most typical—have possessed keen intelligence, and a character not merely strong but lofty, a character exalted by the fact that great power was accompanied by a high and fine determination to use this great power for the common good, for the advancement of mankind. Such men were the builders of New England. As the country grew, such men were the pioneers that pushed the frontiers of civilization westward. A hundred years ago, when men spoke of the West, they meant the country between the Alleghanies and the Mississippi. Fifty years ago the white man's West took in Minnesota, Iowa, and Kansas, and then skipped across to California and Oregon. The country of the great plains and the Rockies has grown up within my own lifetime. I myself saw and took part in the closing years of the pioneer period, and it was my great privilege to work side by side with the pioneers—the ranchmen, the miners, the cow-punchers, the mule-skinners, the bull-whackers—who actually opened up the country. I now travel in every comfort on railways across lands which, when I first rode across them, were still the home of the Indian and the buffalo; and I find cities where one can obtain not merely comfort but luxury, in the places where, thirty years ago, there was not a building beyond a log hut or a 'dobe house. The men who did this work were engaged in the final stages of conquering the continent; and it was their privilege to do one of the great works of all time, to do their part in the performance of an epic feat in the history of the progress of mankind.

The pioneer days are over, save in a few places; and the more complex life of to-day calls for a greater variety of good qualities than were needed on the frontier. There is need at present to encourage the development of new abilities which can be brought to high perfection only by a kind of training useless in pioneer times; but these new qualities can only supplement, and never supplant, the old, homely virtues; the need for the special and distinctive pioneer virtues is as great as ever. In other words, as our civilization grows older and more complex, while it is true that we need new forms of trained ability, and need to develop men whose lives are devoted wholly to the pursuit of special objects, it is yet also true that we need a greater and not a less development of the fundamental frontier virtues.

These qualities, derived from the pioneers, were not confined to the pioneers. They are shown in the deeds of the Nation; and especially in the two great feats which during the past decade have made the deepest impression abroad—the cruise of the battle fleet around the world, and the digging of the Panama Canal.

Now, there is no use of a nation claiming to be a great nation, unless it is prepared to play a great part. A nation such as ours cannot possibly play a great part in international affairs, cannot expect to be treated as of weight in either the Atlantic or the Pacific, or to have its voice as to the Monroe Doctrine or the management of the Panama Canal heeded, unless it has a strong and thoroughly efficient navy. So far from this increase in naval strength representing on our part either a menace of aggression to weaker nations or a menace of war to stronger nations, it has told most powerfully for peace. No nation regarded the cruise as fraught with any menace of hostility to itself; and yet every nation accepted it as a proof that we were not only desirous ourselves to keep the peace, but able to prevent the peace being broken at our expense. No cruise in any way approaching it has ever been made by any fleet of any other Power; and the best naval opinion abroad had been that no such feat was possible; that is, that no such cruise as that we actually made could be undertaken by a fleet of such size without innumerable breakdowns and accidents. The success of the cruise, performed as it was without a single accident, immeasurably raised the prestige, not only of our fleet, but of our Nation; and was a distinct help to the cause of international peace.

As regards the Panama Canal, I really think that outside nations have a juster idea than our own people of the magnitude and success of the work. Six years ago last spring the American Government took possession of the Isthmus. The first two years were devoted to the sanitation of the Isthmus, to assembling the plant and working force, and providing quarters, food, and water supplies. In all these points the success was extraordinary. From one of the plague-spots of the globe, one of the most unhealthy regions in the entire world, the Isthmus has been turned into a singularly healthy place of abode. Active excavation on a large scale did not begin until January, 1907. Three years and a half have gone by since then, and three-fifths of the total excavation has already been accomplished. In 1908 and 1909 the monthly average of rock and earth removed was three million cubic yards, notwithstanding the fact that nine months of each year constituted a season of very heavy rainfall; but it is impossible to maintain such a ratio as the depth increases. Still, it is certain that such a rate can be maintained as will enable the workers to finish the excavation considerably in advance of the date fixed for opening the Canal—January 1, 1915. Indeed, I shall be surprised if the Canal cannot be opened six months or even a year in advance of the time set. The work has two great features: The Culebra Cut, which I have been considering, and the great dam at Gatun. The construction of the dam has advanced sufficiently to convince the engineers in charge of the work of its absolute stability and imperviousness. The engineer in charge has announced that all the concrete in all the locks will be in place two years hence.

This is a stupendous record of achievement. As a people we are rather fond of criticising ourselves, and sometimes with very great justice; but even the most pessimistic critic should sometimes think of what is to our credit. Among our assets of the past ten years will be placed the extraordinary ability, integrity, and success with which we have handled all the problems inherited as the result of the Spanish War; the way we have handled ourselves in the

Philippines, in Cuba, in Porto Rico, in San Domingo, and in Panama. The cruise of the battle fleet around the world was a striking proof that we had made good with the navy; and what we have done at Panama represents the accomplishment of one of the great feats of the ages. It is a feat which reflects the highest honor upon our country; and our gratitude is due to every man who has taken an honorable part in any capacity in bringing it about.

The same qualities that have enabled Americans to conquer the wilderness, and to attempt tasks like the building of the Panama Canal and the sending of the battle fleet around the world, need to be applied now to our future problems; and these qualities, which include the power of self-government, together with the power of joining with others for mutual help, and, what is especially important, the feeling of comradeship, need to be applied in particular to that foremost of National problems, the problem of the preservation of our National resources.

The question has two sides. In the first place, the actual destruction, or, if this is not possible, at any rate the needless waste, of the natural resources must be stopped. In the second place, so far as possible, these resources must be kept for the use of the whole people, and not handed over for exploitation to single individuals or groups of individuals.

The first point I shall not here discuss at length. It is rapidly becoming a well-settled policy of this people that we of the present generation hold the land in part as trustees for the next generation, and not exclusively for our own selfish enjoyment. Just as the farmer is a good citizen if he leaves his farm improved and not impaired to his children, and a bad citizen if he cares nothing for his children and skins the land and destroys its value in his own selfish interest; so the Nation behaves well if it treats the soil and the water and the forests as assets which it must turn over to the next generation increased and not impaired in value, and behaves badly if it leaves the land poorer to those who come after us. No farm should be so used that the soil is permitted to depreciate in value; no forest so used as permanently to impair its productivity.

The second part of the question relates to preserving and using our natural resources in the interest of the public as a whole. We do not intend to discourage individual excellence by improperly diminishing the reward for that individual excellence; on the contrary, our desire is to see that the fullest reward is given to the men of exceptional abilities, up to the point when the abilities are used to the detriment of the people as a whole. We favor the sheep man who feeds his sheep on his own range in such manner that the range increases instead of diminishes in value; and we are against the big man who does not live in the country at all, but who sends migratory bands of sheep with a few hired shepherds to wander over it, destroying pasturage and forests, and seriously impairing the value of the country for actual settlers. We are for the liberty of the individual up to, but not beyond, the point where it becomes inconsistent with the welfare of the community as a whole.

Now, to preserve the general welfare, to see to it that the rights of the public are protected, and the liberty of the individual secured and encouraged as long as consistent with this welfare, and curbed when it becomes inconsistent therewith, it is necessary to invoke the aid of the Government. There are points in which this governmental aid can best be rendered by the States; that is, where the exercise of States' rights helps to secure popular rights, and as to these I believe in States' rights. But there are large classes of cases where only the authority of the National Government will secure the rights of the people, and where this is the case I am a convinced and a thoroughgoing believer in the rights of the National Government. Big business, for instance, is no longer an affair of any one State; big business has become nationalized; and the only effective way of controlling and directing it, and preventing abuses in connection with it, is by having the people nationalize this control in order to prevent their being exploited by the individuals who have nationalized the business. All commerce on a scale sufficiently large to warrant any control over it by Government is nowadays inter-State or foreign commerce; and until this fact is heartily acknowledged, in particular by both courts and legislative bodies, National and State alike, the interest of the people will suffer.

Take the question of the control of the water power sites. The enormous importance of water power sites to the future industrial development of this country has only been realized within a very few years. Unfortunately, the realization has come too late as regards many of the power sites, but many yet remain with which our hands are free to deal. We should make it our duty to see that hereafter the power sites are kept under the control of the general Government for the use of the people as a whole. The fee should remain with the people as a whole, while the use is leased on terms which will secure an ample reward to the lessees, which will encourage the development and use of the water power, but which will not create a permanent monopoly or permit the development to be anti-social, to be in any respect hostile to the public good.

In this country, nowadays, capital has a National and not a State use. The great corporations which are managed and largely owned in the older States are those which are most in evidence in developing and using the mines and water powers and forests of the new Territories and new States, from Alaska to Arizona. I have been genuinely amused during the past two months at having arguments presented to me on behalf of certain rich men from New York and Ohio, for instance, as to why Colorado and other Rocky Mountain States should manage their own water power sites. Now I am sure that those men, according to their lights, are good citizens; but, naturally enough, their special interest obscures their sense of the public need; and as their object is to escape efficient control, they clamor to be put under the State instead of under the Nation. If we are foolish enough to grant their requests, we shall have ourselves to blame when we wake up to find that we have permitted another privilege to intrench itself, and another portion of what should be kept for the public good to be turned over to individuals for purposes of private enrichment.

Our people have for many years proceeded upon the assumption that the Nation controls the public land. The coal should be kept for the people, and those who mine it should pay part of the profit back to the people.

Remember also that many of the men who protest loudly against effective National action would be the first to turn round and protest against the State action if such action in its turn became effective, and would then unhesitatingly invoke the law to show that the State had no Constitutional power to act. I am a strong believer in efficient National action; and if there is one thing which I abhor more than another, it is the creation by legislative, by executive, or by judicial action of a neutral ground in which neither the State nor the Nation has power, and which can serve as a place of refuge for the lawless man, and especially for the lawless man of great wealth, who can hire the best legal counsel to advise him how to keep his abiding-place equally distant from the uncertain frontier of both State and National power.

Let me illustrate what I mean by a reference to two concrete cases. The first is the decision of the United States Supreme Court in the Knight Sugar Trust case. This was really a decision rendering it exceedingly difficult for the people to devise any method of controlling and regulating the business use of great capital in inter-State commerce. It was a decision nominally against National rights, but really against popular rights, against the democratic principle of government by the people.

The second case is the so-called New York Bake-Shop case. In New York City, as in most large cities, the baking business is likely to be carried on under unhygienic conditions, conditions which tell against the welfare of the workers, and therefore against the welfare of the general public. The New York Legislature passed, and the New York Governor signed, a bill remedying these improper conditions. New York State was the only body that could deal with them; the Nation had no power whatever in the matter.

Acting on information which to them seemed ample and sufficient; acting in the interest of the public and in accordance with the demand of the public, the only governmental authority having affirmative power in the matter, the Governor and the Legislature of New York, took the action which they deemed necessary, after what inquiry and study were needed to satisfy them as to the conditions and as to the remedy. The Governor and the Legislature alone had the power to remedy the abuse. But the Supreme Court of the United States possessed, and unfortunately exercised, the negative power of not permitting the abuse to be remedied. By a five to four vote they declared the action of the State of New York unconstitutional. They were, of course, themselves powerless to make the remotest attempt to provide a remedy for the wrong which undoubtedly existed, and their refusal to permit action by the State did not confer any power upon the Nation to act. In effect, it reduced to impotence the only body which did have power, so that in this case the decision, although nominally against State rights, was really against popular rights, against the democratic principle of government by the people under the forms of law.

If such decisions as these two indicated the Court's permanent attitude, there would be real and grave cause of alarm; for such decisions, if consistently followed up, would upset our whole system of popular Government. I am, however, convinced, both from the inconsistency of these decisions with the tenor of other decisions, and furthermore from the very fact that they are in such flagrant and direct contradiction to the spirit and needs of the time, that sooner or later they will be explicitly or implicitly reversed. I mention them merely to illustrate the need of having a truly National system of government under which the people can deal effectively with all problems, meeting those that affect the people as a whole by affirmative Federal action, and those that merely affect the people of one locality by affirmative State action.

In dealing with future problems like this one of Conservation, we need to keep in mind the lesson taught by the American pioneer. It is a lesson that is to be found in the fact that the pioneer is so good an American. He is an American, first and foremost. The man of the West throughout the successive stages of Western growth has always been one of the two or three most typical figures, indeed I am tempted to say the most typical figure, in American life; and no man can really understand our country, and appreciate what it really is and what it promises, unless he has the fullest and closest sympathy with the ideals and aspirations of the West.

The great lesson that all of us need to learn and to keep is the lesson that it is unimportant whether a man lives North or South, East or West, provided that he is genuinely and in good faith an American; that he feels every part of the United States as his own, and that he is honestly desirous to uphold the interests of all other Americans in whatever sections of the country they may dwell.

The Tariff: A Moral Issue

Whenever men just like ourselves—probably not much better, and certainly no worse—continually fail to give us the results we have a right to expect from their efforts, we may just as well make up our minds that the fault lies, not in their personality, but in the conditions under which they work, and profit comes, not from denouncing them, but in seeing that the conditions are changed. This is especially true of tariff-making. It has been conclusively shown, by experiments repeated again and again, that the methods of tariff-making by Congress, which have now obtained for so many years, cannot, from the very nature of the case, bring really satisfactory results. I think that the present tariff is better than the last, and considerably better than the one before the last; but it has certainly failed to give general satisfaction. I believe this country is fully committed to the principle of protection; but it is to protection as a principle; to protection primarily in the interest of the standard of living of the American workingman. I believe that when protection becomes, not a principle, but a privilege and a preference—or, rather, a jumble of privileges and preferences—then the American people disapprove of it. Now, to correct the trouble, it is necessary, in the first place, to get in mind clearly what we want, and, in the next place, to get in mind clearly the method by which we hope to obtain what we want. What we want is a square deal in the tariff as in everything else; a square deal for the wage-earner; a square deal for the employer; and a square deal for the general public. To obtain it we must have a thoroughly efficient and well-equipped tariff commission.

The tariff ought to be a material issue and not a moral issue; but if instead of a square deal we get a crooked deal, then it becomes very emphatically a moral issue. What we desire in a tariff is such measure of protection as will equalize the cost of production here and abroad; and as the cost of production is mainly labor cost, this means primarily a tariff sufficient to make up for the difference in labor cost here and abroad. The American public wants the American laboring man put on an equality with other citizens, so that he shall have the ability to achieve the American standard of living and the capacity to enjoy it; and to do this we must see that his wages are not lowered by improper competition with inferior wage-workers abroad—with wage-workers who are paid poorly and who live as no Americans are willing to live. But the American public does not wish to see the tariff so arranged as to benefit primarily a few wealthy men.

As a means toward the attainment of its end in view we have as yet devised nothing in any way as effective as a tariff commission. There should be a commission of well-paid experts; men who should not represent any industry; who should be masters of their subjects; of the very highest character; and who should approach the matter with absolute disregard of every outside consideration. These men should take up in succession each subject with which the tariff deals and investigate the conditions of production here and abroad; they should find out the facts and not merely accept the statements of interested parties; and they should report to Congress on each subject as soon as that subject has been covered. Then action can be taken at once on the particular subject concerned, while the commission immediately proceeds to investigate another. By these means log-rolling would be avoided and each subject treated on its merits, while there would be no such shock to general industry as is implied in the present custom of making sweeping changes in the whole tariff at once. Finally, it should be the duty of some Governmental department or bureau to investigate the conditions in the various protected industries, and see that the laborers really are getting the benefit of the tariff supposed to be enacted in their interest. Moreover, to insure good treatment abroad we should keep the maximum and minimum provision.

The same principle of a first-class outside commission should be applied to river and harbor legislation. At present a river and harbor bill, like a tariff bill, tends to be settled by a squabble among a lot of big selfish interests and little selfish interests, with scant regard to the one really vital interest, that of the general public. In this matter the National Legislature would do well to profit by the example of Massachusetts. Formerly Massachusetts dealt with its land and harbor legislation just as at Washington tariff and river and harbor laws have been dealt with; and there was just the same pulling and hauling, the same bargaining and log-rolling, the same subordination of the general interest to various special interests. Last year Governor Draper took up the matter, and on his recommendation the Legislature turned the whole business over to a commission of experts; and all trouble and scandal forthwith disappeared. Incidentally, this seems to me to be a first-class instance of progressive legislation.

www.ingramcontent.com/pod-product-compliance
Lightning Source LLC
Chambersburg PA
CBHW021131080526
44587CB00012B/1230